DELUSIONS OF GRAMMAR

DELUSIONS OF GRAMMAR

The Worst of the Worst

Sharon Eliza Nichols

 St. Martin's Griffin   New York

DELUSIONS OF GRAMMAR: I JUDGE YOU WHEN YOU USE POOR GRAMMAR. Copyright © 2009 by Sharon Eliza Nichols. MORE BADDER GRAMMAR! Copyright © 2011 by Sharon Eliza Nichols. All rights reserved. Printed in China. For information, address St. Martin's Press, 175 Fifth Avenue, New York, N.Y. 10010.

www.stmartins.com

The Library of Congress Cataloging-in-Publication Data is available upon request.

ISBN 978-1-250-12151-6 (trade paperback)

Our books may be purchased in bulk for promotional, educational, or business use. Please contact your local bookseller or the Macmillan Corporate and Premium Sales Department at 1-800-221-7945, extension 5442, or by e-mail at MacmillanSpecialMarkets@macmillan.com.

First Edition: January 2017

10 9 8 7 6 5 4 3 2 1

I JUDGE YOU WHEN YOU

USE POOR GRAMMAR

For my parents, who love me even when I don't deserve it,

and for my brother and sister,

who are capable of far more than they know.

CONTENTS

PREFACE

As evidenced by the three hundred thousand plus members of the Facebook group by the same name, I'm not alone in my contempt of the misuse of the English language. I judge people when they use poor grammar, you judge people when they use poor grammar, and we've probably all been the unknowing recipient of some other grammarian's judgment of our (extraordinarily rare, of course) poor uses of grammar.

Words are the foundation of our interaction with each other. They communicate definite impressions to other people, and this is especially true for writing aimed at large audiences, such as the advertising of big companies or traffic signs on four-lane highways. You've probably seen signs like those in the following pages and thought to yourself, "Somebody should have known better!"

Spelling and grammatical errors are far too common, but fortunately, the members of the Facebook group have a sense of humor. These enthusiastic grammar groupies have taken and uploaded some seven thousand pictures of signs with errors that capture outrageous grammatical, spelling, and usage mistakes that appear in prominent places. This book is a collection of the funniest and most ridiculous of those pictures. I hope you enjoy the book as much as I enjoyed putting it together.

ACKNOWLEGMENTS

First and foremost, I'm grateful for the providence of God. Thank you to my grandparents, who have loved and encouraged me over the years. I'm also appreciative of the many coaches and teachers whose love and support shaped me into the person I am.

I'm thankful for Neil Salkind, my agent, and my editor, Daniela Rapp, both of whom graciously tolerated my procrastination and taught me how to create a book. (Neil and Daniela, my parents also thank you—from their hearts and their wallets.)

Thank you to the people at University of Alabama School of Law who had faith in me and helped throughout this process. Specifically, Aaron Latham and Professors Scott England, Alfred Brophy, and Paul Horwitz all contributed in different ways to making this book achievable.

Thank you to David Lat, who gave me my first shot at writing professionally. Finally, I'd like to extend my gratitude to Helen, Josh, Nick, Paco, Justin, Robert, Gloria, and Stephanie, and to all the members of the Facebook group who captured the images in this book. I hope the final result lives up to all of your expectations.

(P.S.: If I left anyone out, my bad. Send the hate mail to the Facebook grammar group!)

One
∧

FOOD
AND
DRINK

It's the Southern take on the French Bistro.

But evidently alcohol was allowed while creating the sign.

Yum, bowels and camels early in the morning!

It plugs up the sink and wastes precious coffee grinds.

Apparently, this is a common mistake. The plural of knife is knives.

Is the fish Chip's
or are the chips Chip's?

We're here, we want the early dinner special,
get used to it. And don't leave off the pickels!

Their hot what?

I need my apostrophe eraser. And my Z flipper.

Tea isn't coffee, right?

So close to what you meant, but now I really want to see the writer of this sign curtsey while fixing it.

Pick a spelling, any spelling.

Opposite: I shouldn't have to contemplate apostrophes while waiting for my arteries to harden.

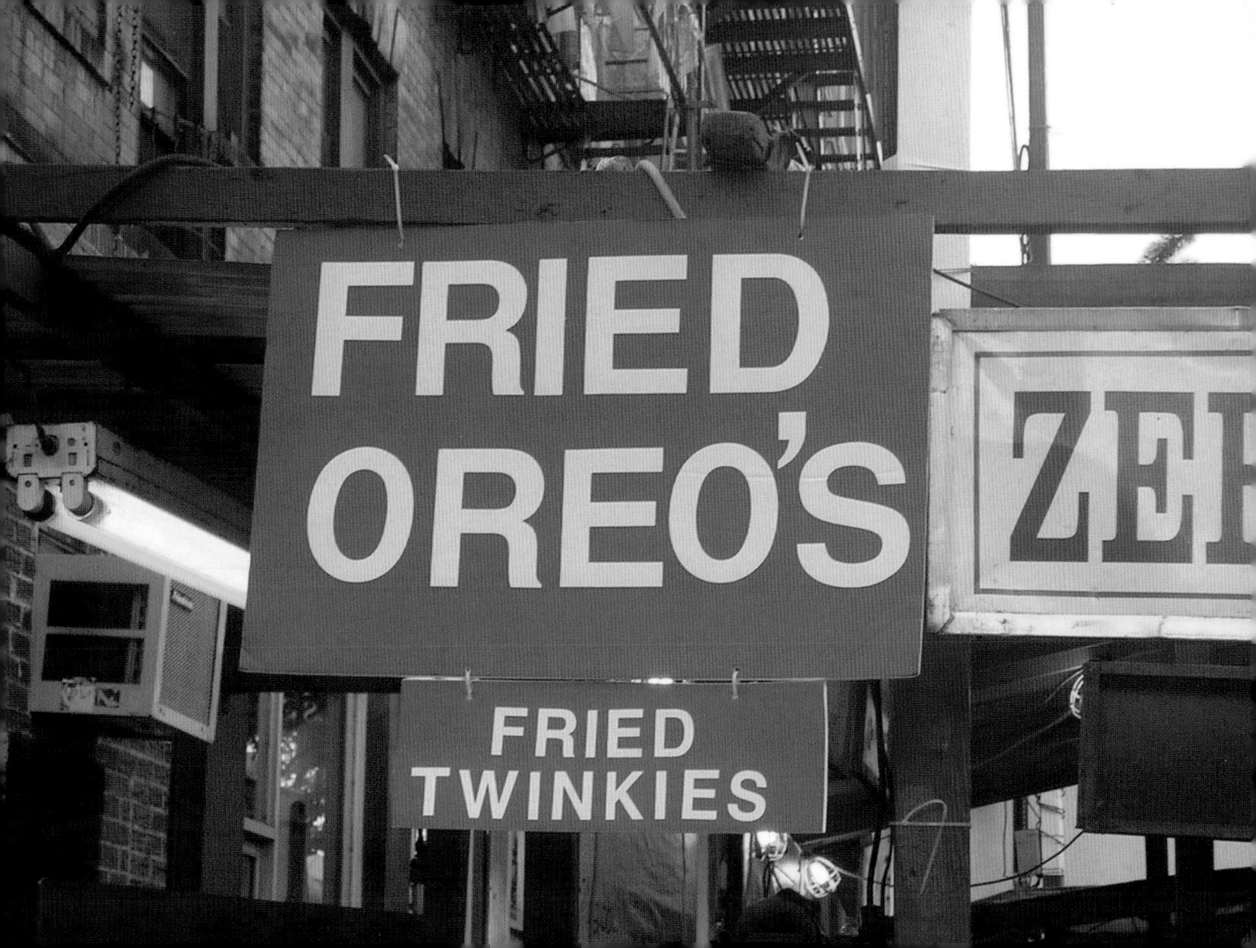
FRIED
OREO'S
FRIED
TWINKIES

Don't let bad punctuation happen to good neon.

I hope they all went to ooking school.

Cheese! It *does* not come included.

THERE BACK
CHICKEN FLAUTAS
STARTING AT $2 99
DT OPEN 24 HOURS

We take everything BUT reservations here!

Does this juice taste like metal to you?

Opposite: *They're back* sounds far more ominous than it's used here.

Katie's legal! Now, the difference between *your* and *you're*. . . .

No apostrophe. For the last time: Apostrophe for possession, just an *s* to make something plural.

Go ahead, cheesecake, make them happy!

Come on and git it!

Take the bad apostrophe away and make the poor man happy!

Hole Weet bread for sale. I prefer mine without holes and only very little weet, thanks.

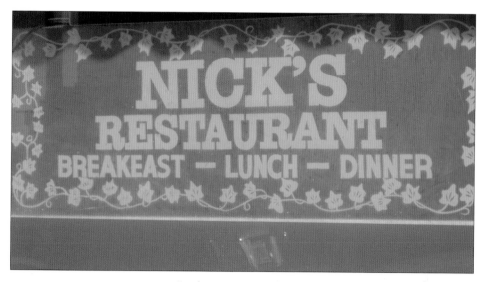

Breakeast versus Breakwest?

Two
∧

SHOPPING
SIGNAGE

Well, it is much easier to spell than bouquet.

This is a error.

Dad's gets an apostrophe, but not *grads*. They couldn't even make consistent mistakes.

Ipod's what are available here?

As a beauty store, shouldn't you know how to spell *aesthetics*? Especially if you want to name your store "Salon & Aesthetics."

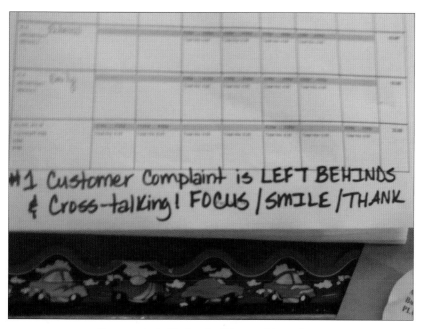

Those pesky behinds—don't leave without them.

Life's too short to struggle with which two to use. Learn it.

No, no, NO. We will not attend your yard sael, your yard sail, or even your yard sayle.

Ouch. Spelling mistakes can have painful results, kids.

You *are* local express store, and you *will* be open as normal. And you *will* use an apostrophe for possessives.

Opposite: Wanna buy an *o*?

At least it's not laminated.

There's more than one Brett?
The Cubby owns the toys?

APPLY FOR A FREE SAM'S CREDIT CARDS AND GET A FREE KEY LIME BUNDT CAKE TODAY THAT'S CORRECT THEY BOTH ARE FREE

No punctuation? Perhaps that's how the store can give things away for free. Expensive periods and commas!

Your stylin? So the style is yours? Now your talkin'.

Opposite: Horrible what happens when your apostrophe drops.

Its newest stars. Its. *It's* means *it is*.

You got people? I have people, thanks.

Three
∧

FASHION
STATEMENTS

Put this T-shirt in the trash.

Our worst nightmare: a missing apostrophe.

Teaching babies the wrong places to
put apostrophes is child abuse.

It's not cheating if your drunk cousin does it? Ohh, if *you're* drunk. Say what you mean, kids.

Oops! Some mistakes are worse than others.

I ♥ the proper use of apostrophes.

No, no, no, no! *Want* does *not* want an apostrophe!

Four

∧

PARKING, DRIVING, CARS, AND TRAVEL

Does *privite* rhyme with *invite*?

Has anyone seen two missing *E*'s?

Don't drink and make road signs.

If the bus brakes, the glass
brakes as well.

DEPARTMENT OF HOMELAND SECURITY
U.S. Customs and Border Protection

OMB No. 1651-0113

Welcome to the United States

I-94W Nonimmigrant Visa Waiver Arrival/Departure Form
Instructions

This form is to be completed by every nonimmigrant visitor not in possession of a visitor's visa, who is a national of one of the countries enumerated in 8 CFR 217. The airline can provide your with the current list of eligible countries.

Type or print legibly with pen in ALL CAPITAL LETTERS. **USE ENGLISH**

This form is in two parts. Please complete both the Arrival Record, items **1** through **11** and the Departure Record, items **14** through **17**. The reverse side of this form must be signed and dated. Children under the age of fourteen must have their form signed by a parent/guardian.

Item 7 - If you are entering the United States by land, enter **LAND** in this space. If you are entering the United States by ship, enter **SEA** in this space.

This is one of the first things visitors see upon entering the United States. You'd think that the grammar and punctuation would be impeccable, right? Provide your what?

Blind drivers, corner slowly. Drivers who can see, corner at full speed.

The gate is closed, people. *Closed*.

So the cars park themselves?

Kids without gas have to sit in the car.

Canada *cannot* fit in a suitcase.

You could have saved yourself some space on this sign!

The road less traveled, probably to your right.

Just because you pronounce it that way
doesn't mean it's spelled that way.

"Please remain seated until tender is dock." Hmm. "Please remain seated until the dock is tendered?" Who knows?

You'd think traffic signals painted on the ground should be spelled correctly. Especially a word like *parking*.

ENTERING FEE AREA
Trail Pass Required

Visit Sundance
Mountain Outfitters
For Pass

With Pass, Trails Open
10 AM - 6:30 PM Daily

VIOLATORS WILL BE
TRESPASSED

We wonder what being trespassed would feel like.

Parking quietly, however, is allowed.

I before *E,* except after *C*. Write that one hundred times over while you *think* about what you've done.

Five
∧

NEWSPAPERS AND BOOKS

PHOTO COURTESY OF CHRYSLER LLC

Dodge has upgraded teh interior of the new Ram.

Proofreader on vacation?

C'mon, people. You work at a newspaper, you should know better!

Either the magazines are kind, or there should be an *s* at the end of *kind*. And *magazines*.

Even the news store needs to relearn the apostrophe chapter from 2nd grade.
We're disappointed in you, Hearsall.

There should probably be some punctuation in that bottom line.

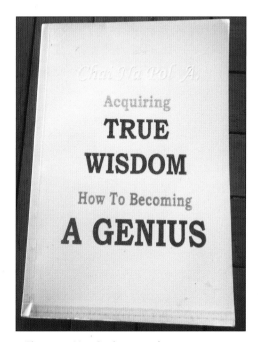

First step: Hey Genius—watch your grammar.

Six
∧

EDUMACATION

Well, it's only Junior High—there's still time to learn the difference between *your* and *you're*.

Vive l'indépendance!

Is there a spelling category for the Wolverine achievement awards?

Student government needs a grammar check.

EXHIBITING PAINTINGS

ALMOST EVERY PAINTER ARRIVES AT THE STAGE WHEN HE WOULD LIKE TO EXHIBIT HIS WORK. IT IS A GOOD IDEA TO HAVE YOUR PAINTINGS SHOWN WITH THOSE OF OTHERS, IT GIVES YOU A FRESH PERSPECTIVE ON YOUR WORK. BECAUSE IT IS SURPRISING HOW DIFFERENT YOUR PICTURES LOOK ON THE WALL SURROUNDED BY PAINTINGS OF OTHER ARTISTS. SOMETIMES YOU ARE AGREEABLY SURPRISED WHEN YOUR PAINTING HOLDS ITS OWN IN COMPARISON. AT OTHER TIMES THE PAINTING THAT SEEMED SO COLORFUL AND STRONG IN YOUR STUDIO LOOKS DRAB AND WEAK ALONGSIDE OTHER PICTURES.

You'd think the Museum of Modern Art in Washington, DC, would double-check for grammatical mistakes.

Teaching children bad punctuation is unacceptable.

Consistency aside, this is still wrong.

No excetions, eh? How about learning to spell *exceptions?*

Spirt? Wonder what they're spirting.

Seven

∧

LOST

IN

TRANSLATION

Good luck in Mexico! Correct English grammar,
but a shabby translation at best.

I sale, you sale, we sale . . . stams?

Don't tripe when you're
drunkenly walking.

This has got to be the wittiest
restroom I have ever seen.

The speech delay will appreciate the free classes, we're sure.

Don't get kicked; take care of your hind!

Someone made a stamp that says "Norrh"?

Somebody paid for this sign.

Oh, of course. Restrooms are
toward your behind.

Somebody call Dateline!

Watch out for the slippery trip hazard.

Where *should* the brown paper go?

Bewere, but happy dining!

It's a holy place. Leave your
cigarettes and guns outside.

Coming soon: Java Judo. You're
wellcome to that also.

Enjoy me as much as you want.

This sign brought to you from Thaisland.

All together now: "to be, or not to be" broken.

因重要活动，给您的参观游览带来不便，敬请原谅。

Because the important activity, is gone on a sightseeing tour by you bring about forgiving inconveniently, please.

故宫博物院
The Palace Museum

Exhibits like sightseeing as much everyone else.

Eight

SAY

WHAT?

I am so scared of poltergiests. There and back.

"Claw don't move foreward nor backward."
At least the apostrophe is correct.

This dryer *doesn't* heat up.

If you're tored, you're unvalid.

A case of the mix-and-match vowel syndrome.

They're removing the beach?

Unfortunately, we think this one was on purpose.

George must be gorgeous.

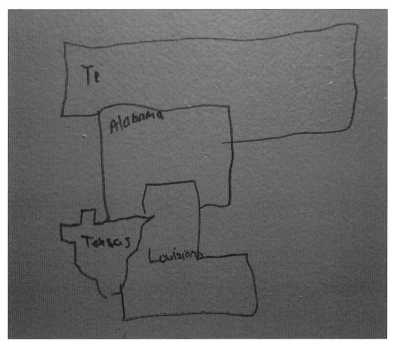

Nice drawing; unfortunate spelling.

Isn't spell check automatic when you type signs?

That sign be broke, too.

I stopped reading, thank goodness.

The adverb is dying. Use *ly*, people, before it disappears completely.

Protect hurricanes and global warming
while you're at it.

Everythings's cheap! And
hopelessly incorrect!

What do you think a "personnel
watermelon" is?

So, in other words, someone is getting very near for an event involving running. But it's ok, no need to be sorry for something so in convenience.

The quotation marks do not make
us trust this store.

We don't know what he's trying to say, but we
do know that *globle* and *analisis* aren't words.

Don't knock it 'til you've tried it.

Well, hotdawhg!

You're freacking us out here.

"Frow papers int the basket." Got that?

LaConner Fire Dept.
THNX FOR TELING US
ABOT R SPELUN
MIZTAKES NOW WE NO
SUMONE IS READIN R SINE

Glad someone is listening!

Nine
Λ

APOSTROPHE
CATASTROPHE

Free kids! And their coloring, we suppose.

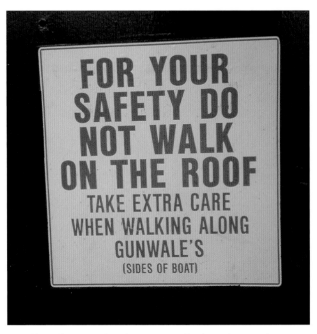

Also take care when it comes to plurals and possessives.

Please return smokers and blankets to this basket when you're through with them.

These forty-eight cents belong to the bananas!

Go have a shot of whiskey. Your grammar needs help.

We think they meant *parties*.

This toilet must be for one specific boy.

Please, just use any of the abundant extra apostrophes from this chapter.

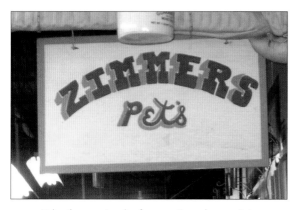

I'm in a hurry to fix that
bastardized *your're*.

Take the apostrophe from *pet's* and move it to
Zimmer's. Much better.

Mow'in Joe's
Lawn Cutting

$35.00 a cut
Includes:
mowing, weekwacking,
and blowing off
driveway and walkway

Does Joe mow or does the service mow Joe? Why is there an apostrophe in the middle of *mowin'*? And how do you wack a week?

Apostrophe eraser please? *Tellers*. That's better.

This sign is full of opportunities to correct its punctuation.

PLEASE TUCK YOU'RE LACES IN THANK YOU

You are laces? Really now. That's interesting.

This sign makes us think we haven't progressed all that much since the pirates.

We're having visions of Dr. Seuss's Whos.

Ten
∧

MISCELLANEOUS

Welcomme to this bar! Come in and get a free apostrophe!

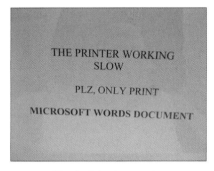

Slowly. Adverbs, people.

Natalie and Mark was here. Or were here. Whatever.

There's no spelling test for voting, thank goodness.

Pray for the birds of prey.

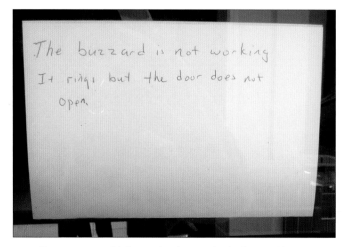

Everyone, you didn't pray hard enough, the buzzard is not working. The buzzer, however, is of questionable status.

We hope this sign was on sale (or on sael).

If you have this sign in front of your house, you might be a redneck.

You can block the door closed, but not open.

This is another lamination abomination.

Even your dog and cat are making faces at your incompetent spelling. Very unproffessional!

FOR YOU'RE EYES ONLY!
PLEASE!
DO NOT TOUCH THE BIRD'S
THEY WILL BITE YOU!

The birds will bite you, since you are all eyes. And don't touch the bird's what?

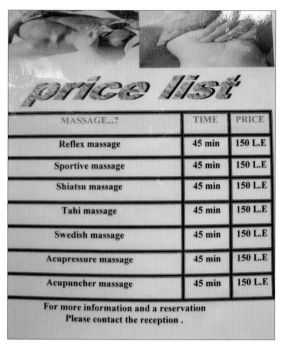

MASSAGE...?	TIME	PRICE
Reflex massage	45 min	150 L.E
Sportive massage	45 min	150 L.E
Shiatsu massage	45 min	150 L.E
Tahi massage	45 min	150 L.E
Swedish massage	45 min	150 L.E
Acupressure massage	45 min	150 L.E
Acupuncher massage	45 min	150 L.E

For more information and a reservation
Please contact the reception .

You puncher, you brought her.

As opposed to a
non-male man?

The beach does what?

Waving the sign won't distract us from the woefully inadequate grammar featured on it.

We'd rather not suffocate while watching TV.

Get spell check, dude!

PHOTO CREDITS

Andrew Albertson: 110 (right)
Trish Amee: 133 (left)
Michelle Arney: 9 (right)
Marianne Baker: 79 (left)
Amanda Brzezowski: 124 (left)
Kristin Burke: 21
Megan Jayne Butler: 75 (left)
Brittany Candeger: 29
Kevin Challenger: 36
Michelle Cosper: 91 (left)
Lori Crichter: 3
Christopher Curzio: 8, 121 (right)
Lisa Davis: 16 (right)
Amy Dee: 130
Elaine K. de la Mata: 136
Mary Dempsey: 25
Octavio Diaz: 103
Steve Dinn: 75 (left)
Alan Duda: 46
Danielle Dumanoir: 138 (left)

Jessica Rachel Dunlop: 19, 63, 95
Rowena Evans: 35 (top)
Tiffany Fox: 79 (right), 94 (left)
Kira Gaber: 142 (left)
Samantha Garofalo: 91 (right)
Kelly Gilbert: 112 (right), 116 (right)
Lauren Gray: 114
Amy Griffin: 100 (right)
Karrie Guthrie: 44, 137 (right),
    143 (left)
Matthew B. Harnick: 142 (right)
Paul Harrison: 69
Carly Heims: 11, 12, 89
Meredith Hilliard: 47, 140
Ben Hogenauer: 134 (right)
Becky Hughes: 57
Thomas Humphries: 31 (right)
Emily Hunt: 88
Allison Hussey: 43
Samantha Iyer: 15 (right), 102 (left)

Juliet Jackson: 110 (left)
Sara Jenkins: 7 (right)
Kathryn Johnston: 84
Annie Jones: 5 (right)
Lauren K. Keller: 135
Richard Kessler: 144
Kashif Siddiq Khawaja: 111
John King: 60
Michael Kirshner: 10 (right)
Tony Klose: 9 (left), 26 (left)
Rebecca Koger: 104
Todd Lanouette: 106 (left)
Jeanne LaSala: 92
Andy Lawson: 45, 55 (right)
Nancy Little: 32
Mara Lopez: 56
E. C. MacGregor Boyle: 139
Jodie Madsen: 62 (right)
Michel Marizco: 83
Virginia Minehart: 115

MORE BADDER GRAMMAR!

CONTENTS

ACKNOWLEDGMENTS

Thank you to all the dedicated group members who submitted photos a second time around. Your pictures made the time spent putting this book together incredibly enjoyable.

Specifically: April Kolin for your "no school" picture, Elizabeth Gunnells for catching the pet store "experimenting" on the goldfish, Francisco Reyes for spotting the "stollen" dog, Jeremy J. Kruizenga for pointing out yet another Taco Bell Fail, Maritxu de Alaiza for the "RRZ RRZ RZZ," and Michael Kirchner for your many, many hilarious submissions. Even if I didn't mention you I thoroughly enjoyed looking through all of your pictures. Thank you for your services, as you courageously defended the Grammar Nation by keeping your cameras ready to shoot the grammatical offenders.

Thank you to my editor Daniela, who is always patient and helps me clarify my somewhat-spastic sense of humor into coherent writing. These books would not exist without you.

Thanks to my friends who have supported me during a very difficult year: Chandler Thomas, whose Twitter account never fails to entertain (and is always grammatically perfect); Elaine Savarese, whose Hall & Oates musical I dream about seeing; Joe Quinn, who selflessly gave me his room for the summer; Anna Zoeller, who will leave us to get her Ph.D. in English soon; Katie Abney, who I fully expect to see running a major magazine one day; Ryan Wilson, who will be walking me down the aisle at some point in the future (as a friend or as the groom has yet to be determined); Helen Van Wagoner, for whom I will gladly wear a purple bridesmaid dress; Chase Espy, who undoubtedly will be known as Judge Espy one day; Gloria Son, whose biting wit and feathered hair will always make me smile; Grace Nichols, my sister and best friend, for tagging me in your solo pics. Everyone else, you know who you are.

To my brother, who passed away this year, entirely too soon: I'm a better person because of the two months we had in Charleston. I love you, and I know that when you invented basketball you never dreamed it'd get this big.

To my sister and parents: Thank you, I love you, and it will get better.

One
∧
BUSINESS AS USUAL

Alpine Sports now has two convenient locations for all your ski rento
needs! Our newest location is in the Parkway Plaza just steps for Cit
Liquors and City Market! And we still offer a Ski Rental Shuttle directl
to your holiday home. We will pick you up and take you to Alpin
Sports and deliver you back to your door. If you are in need of acce
sories and ski clothing, we have a huge **selection** to choose from.

Two locations conveniently located at the intersection of Main St. & Ridge St.,
and in the Parkway Shopping Plaza with plenty of parking available.

70.453.8100

It's understandable to get "form" and "from" mixed up, but substituting "for" is borderline ridiculous.

(2)

"Tetanus" must have that "a" in the middle. Otherwise — combined with the electronic lights — this sign is reminiscent of Tetris, the admittedly awesome video game.

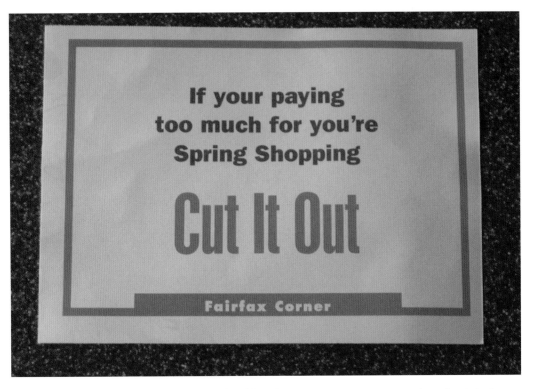

**If your paying
too much for you're
Spring Shopping**

Cut It Out

Fairfax Corner

Whoever made this sign should cut it out, e.g., cut out two words and switch them.

Congratulation's to our Agua Fria Store a
Total of $7,409.75! Congratulation's to C
All of you for your hard work in making t
a goal of $60,000.00, and just fell short of
meet $60,000.00!

Congratulations on [not] understanding the possessive form.

Please don't. You clearly have other things to worry about.

The creator of this sign needs a remedial sixth-grade English course.

We're not aware of "his'n" ever being accept-able, even in the coarsest slang.

Gangsters should know how to spell. Otherwise they are much less intimidating.

If you bought either of these shirts, do the world a favor and don't get any more tattoos. And please don't have any more children.

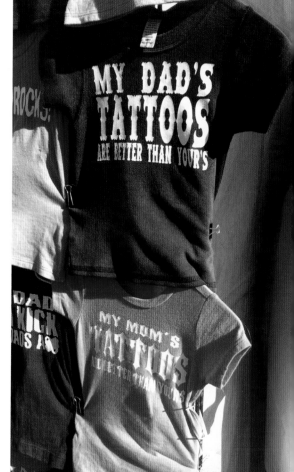

THE WORLDS ONLY PROTECTIVE SHEET

Q: WHATS THE DIFFERENCE BETWEEN A FLY SHEET & A PROTECTIVE SHEET?

A: PIECE OF MIND.

FIND U

WWW.KENSINGTONPRODUCTS.COM

This poor animal is wearing a picnic tablecloth in a horribly written ad.
It's probably better that its eyes are covered.

The world would be a better place if TVs had spell check.

Doesn't experimenting on animals usually take place in labs, not pet stores?

Salon & Café
$40 HAIR CUTS
TUESDAY'S & WEDNESDAY'S

Something that appears twice in this banner needs to be cut.

At least this person was consistently wrong.

Blue Water Bay Employees
Must Wash Your Hands
Before Leaving!

The service at this establishment is clearly superior. You don't even have to wash your own hands.

Isn't there spell check on the software used to make banners? Or common sense in the people who make them?

Comming Soon Nail Salon

You'd think if a person can spell "affordability" correctly they'd know the difference between "its" and "it's."

"Wardreobe." That's a fun new word.

PLACE TRAY'S HERE

PLEASE REFRAIN FROM PUTTING THESE ITEMS IN THE TRASH CANS

Earth Fare
market & café

Please refrain from using unnecessary apostrophes. Thanks.

Two

∧

SKOOLED

There should be a state law forbidding misspelled words on government property.

Maybe they should rethink canceling school that day.

This doesn't bode well for the future of Texas education.

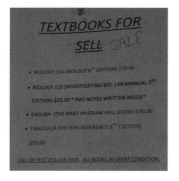

One of those textbooks probably shows the difference between the words "sell" and "sale." Maybe instead of selling them, you should reread them.

Dear Lord, please don't let this man get elected.

This must be an incredibly small school.

Do we really need to prove it?

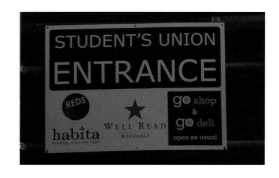

Poor public-speaking class. It must have cankles.

Instead of a student union for hanging out, this school should have more classrooms. You know, for learning.

This might be excusable—if an elementary school student put it up. Somehow we doubt that was what happened.

Three
∧
TALKING OBJECTS

Are the contents of this box something else pretending to be a shelf?

The bald eagle soaring over the snow-capped mountains says "thank you" to the nurses and staff of St. Charles Hospital. Why? Only he knows.

What did you do to alarm the door? And why would you want to upset it?

THIS DOOR IS NOW
ALARMED

Use only in the case of an *emergency*.

This pamphlet is practically on its knees begging you to answer its question. It is apparently speaking.

There are several possibilities here:

- The sign is using quotation marks ironically, so it's actually not sorry that no pets are allowed. It hates animals, anyway.

- The sign itself is embarrassed that somebody forced it to display the rule against pets, so it's apologizing to potentially upset petlovers. If the sign had its way, pets would be welcome.

- The sign creator doesn't know what quotation marks mean.

Ironic quotation marks or fake computers?

Four

^

HIGH TECH

clockDSCN5304BW.jpg

clockDSCN5305BW.jpg

File:

cloc

cloc

cloc

Import to internal memory? If the same file has already been added, the file is overwritten.

cloc

cloc

cloc

Yes | No

clockDSCN5305BW.jpg
11/Feb/2010   3.281 MB
3648x2736

Something in this picture needs to be overwrited.

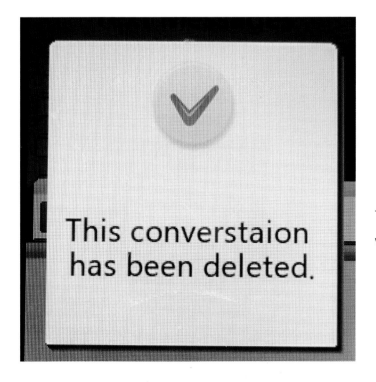

This is almost another new word: converstaion.

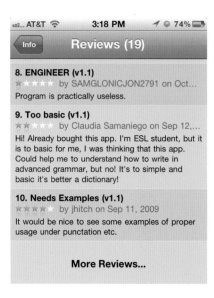

These are the reviews from a grammar iPhone application (which we won't name).

Commas and apostrophes are *not* interchange-able, and even if they were this would still be incorrect.

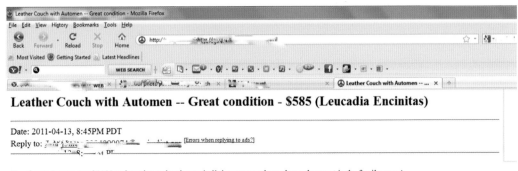

Leather Couch with Automen -- Great condition - $585 (Leucadia Encinitas)

Date: 2011-04-13, 8:45PM PDT
Reply to: [Errors when replying to ads?]

Brand new 5 years ago $2150 and rarely used as it was in living room and we always hung out in the family room!

does not have recliners, its a 4 piece sectional with each unit with a slight angle so as it fits together creates a arc as seen in the second picture

Selling because moving.

- Location: Leucadia Encinitas
- it's NOT ok to contact this poster with services or other commercial interests

http://sandiego.craigslist.org/ssd/fuo/2324056464.html

The lack of intelligible copy on this ad is almost as impressive as the "automen" in

the posting's title. Quick! Free-associate: Automen. Ottoman. Automatic ottoman?

verizonwireless

Phones | Plans | Accessories | Entertainment & Apps | Messaging | Support | My Verizon

THANK YOU FOR YOUR INTEREST IN VERZION WIRELESS.

Verizon Wireless offers a large selection of the latest phones. Here are some recommendations to help you pick out the perfect one for your needs.

Continue Shopping

Haven't quite found what you are looking for?

All Phones ›
Smartphones ›
Internet Devices ›
Accessories ›

Samsung Fascinate
★★★★☆
(read 421 reviews)* *

2-yr Contract Price	$299.99
Online Discount	-$100.00
Your Price	$199.99*

Other Popular Devices

Motorola DROID 2
★★★★☆
(read 768 reviews)*

2-yr Contract Price	$299.99
Online Discount	-$100.00
Your Price	$199.99*

HTC DROID INCREDIBLE
★★★★☆
(read 3,024 reviews)*

2-yr Contract Price	$299.99
Online Discount	-$100.00
Your Price	$199.99*

BlackBerry Bold 9550 smartphone
★★★★☆
(read 548 reviews)*

2-yr Contract Price	$249.99
Online Discount	-$100.00
Your Price	$149.99*

* Based on customer reviews as of 10/26/2010. New 2-YR renewal req'd. 3G multimedia phones require voice plan with data pack $9.99 or higher. 3G Smartphones require voice plan with data pack

---

We have a sneaking suspicion that whoever created this ad was fired. They spelled the name of the company wrong.

Five

∧

QUESTIONABLE INTENTIONS

This penny-smashing machine has something in common with many, many Americans right now.

From what we can tell, the bottom line was supposed to say "we sale Sunday bear." Oh, okay.

This company might brew excellence only during the last weekend of July or only during the last week at the end of July. Although either interpretation doesn't make much sense.

It's a good guess to say that this was intentional.

The more important question: Why?

The two possible interpretations of this are pretty obvious. Either way, we will not be visiting this establishment.

Clearly unintentional, and oddly sweet.

Ah, witty replies to bathroom graffiti always make us smile.

The intended verb in the second line of the description gives us pause.

The unintentionally ironic quotation marks strike again.

Claiming you're perfect is a dangerous game.

We'd like to meet this guy named Wing.

My, my, technology certainly has become advanced.

Honk if you're judging this guy!

We're pretty sure badass ladies also know how to spell "bad."

Do the bras own the ladies?

What's the landlord wanted for? And should he be dead or alive?

The door is also a lock? Are doors and locks the same thing now?

Six
∧
TRANSPORTATION, TRAVEL, & LEISURE

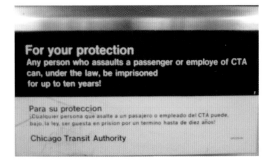

Please:
For you and your pet's
protection, and
the safety of other
travelers
and their pet's,
make certain your
pet is on a leash.

Two different uses of "pet," yet consistent apostrophe use. One of these is wrong.

For your protection
Any person who assaults a passenger or employe of CTA
can, under the law, be imprisoned
for up to ten years!

Para su proteccion
¡Cualquier persona que asalte a un pasajero o empleado del CTA puede,
bajo la ley, ser puesta en prision por un termino hasta de diez años!

Chicago Transit Authority

We'd argue that the person who created this sign deserves jail time.

How many violators?

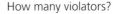

Apparently many people don't know how to make a word possessive.

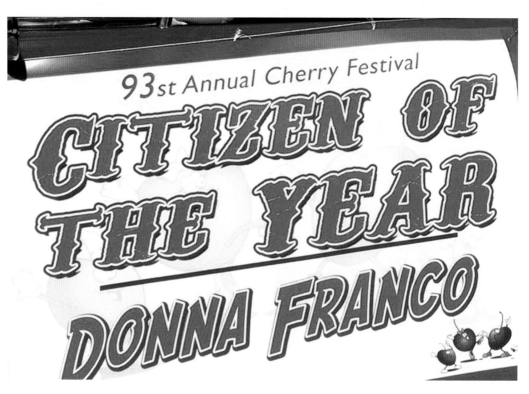

93st Annual Cherry Festival

CITIZEN OF THE YEAR

DONNA FRANCO

Imagining how one would pronounce "93st" is highly amusing.

Please do not bring ski's of any kind into the unit.

The possessive strikes again. We wonder if this is the most confusing part of the English language for native speakers.

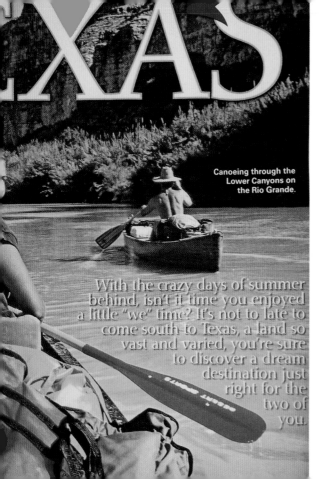

Canoeing through the Lower Canyons on the Rio Grande.

With the crazy days of summer behind, isn't it time you enjoyed a little "we" time? It's not to late to come south to Texas, a land so vast and varied, you're sure to discover a dream destination just right for the two of you.

When the purpose of your business is to publish written works, you should probably have the "to"/"too"/"two" distinction down pat.

LOCAL AREA INFORMATION

Local Hotel's

There are numerous Hotels' of all types within 30 minutes of Lackland AFB. Those mentioned herein are listed due to their convenient proximity to the base. This is not an endorsement of their products.

This person tried it two different ways in this ad and neither succeeded. Maybe the third time's the charm.

This person misspelled "vacuum." But far more troubling is the fact that there's a vacuum by this free-standing jail cell. We won't even ask why.

This could be your tax dollars at work, folks.

This would be funnier if it were "parks and recreatoin."

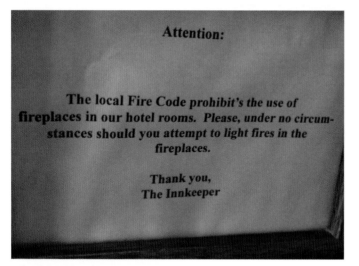

Who cares about incorrect possessives? Just DO NOT, UNDER ANY CIRCUMSTANCES, light a fire in your fireplace.

This sign was created in response to the great paring epidemic of 2010.

This guy gets extra points for the "Khan" pun, which are immediately cancelled out by the missing apostrophe in "cant."

A rolling stone gathers no moss.

That's an inventive use of the number 1. May we buy a real vowel, please?

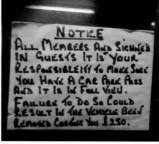

Sports team allegiances are hardcore. Apparently hatred of one's rival can cause brain cramps, shortness of breath, and blindness.

It is "your" responsibility. And we applaud "your" failed effort of creating a noun by adding "ity" to "responsible."

After reading this we can't help imagining 100 human "feets" lined up as a measuring tool.

Let's blame this one on the alcohol.

Take a hike. No, seriously.

Seven
∧
REALLY? REALLY.

Redundancy anyone, anyone?

But wait… isn't smoking bad for you?

TO HELP REDUCE

WAITING TIME IN LINE;

PLEASE HAVE ALL FORMS

COMPLETED AND

PACKAGES READY FOR

MAILING, BEFORE

YOU ARRIVE AT THE

COUNTER FOR SERVICE.

Unnecessary punctuation probably hurts your eyes as much as it does ours.

They were on the right track here…

This sign illustrates another problem America is facing: the disappearance of the adverb. Please, do your part to save the adverbs.

We think the dog ran away on its own.

This flyer looks like the result of putting text into a cheap online translator then mixing it with a four-year-old's spelling.

It appears Flava-Flav has gone green. He's sponsoring his own vegetables now.

Aside from the unnecessary apostrophe, this sign at a chiropractor's office is probably not politically correct.

Okay, maybe they ran out of room on the first line. But wow, that's an expensive

chicken tender meal. And they also ran out of "o"s?

What is a "beverage tapper container"?

CARE INSTRUCTIONS FOR ICE TEA BEVERAGE TAPPER CONTAINER

Prior to using this product, you should wash it in warm soapy water, using a mild detergent. When the plastic lid is firmly secured, you may pour directly from the container by flipping the lid vent open. inside nut in a clockwise rotation, Press, and release the spigot plunger to assure its Be sure to tighten the spigot by hand turning the proper positioning. **Caution: Never pour boiling or extremely hot liquid into the container, and never place the container over an open fire, or other heating element. In addition, never use this product in a microwave oven.**

For general cleaning, remove the plunger, and rinse with clean water, Do not remove the spigot, or rubber gasket encircling the hole,Do not use a scouring pad on the glass suface, Use only a sponge and mild detergent.**Caution: Never use this product in a dish washer**

When using this product to prepare ice tea, always be sure the lid is securely tightened before lifting witn lid handle. Occasionally, heat fron the sun can loosen the lid. Always hold the jar with both hands when lifting, and never lift with the handle alone. To prevent scratching, use only non-metallic utensils in the glass jar.

This beverage container is made of top - quality materials, and is designed for your convenience, We hope that you will enjoy using your beverage tapper container.

Perhaps this is forgivable because it was made by a young Girl Scout troop. But where were their parents?

This banner illustrates why you should always carry a Sharpie. It's deserving of some guerilla justice, grammar Nazi-style.

Where have all the adverbs gone?

There seems to be a theme here.

> **TO OUR VALUED CUSTOMERS**
>
> One of our escalators are out of order, still waiting for the special part to fix, Please walk or use the elevator when needed. Sorry for any inconvenience it may have cause.

At least this sign is very polite, if very ungrammatical.

A Google search of the word "aprons" reveals that this misspelling is apparently a common mistake. How disheartening.

Oh! That's what a sneez gard is.

The early bird should use her extra time to study grammar.

I wish that you could spell.

For the Childrens safety strictly no pedestrian access Please use the main entrance

For the children's edification, please use proper punctuation.

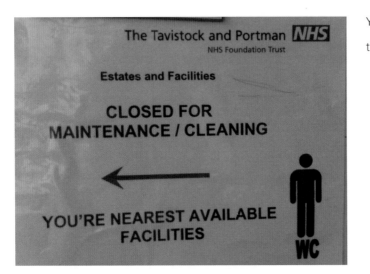

You are nearest available facilities. Oh, thanks.

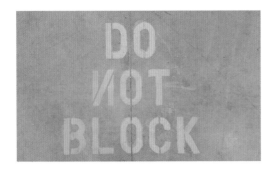

This had to be on purpose, right? Or maybe the stencilbearer is Russian.

Eight

IN OTHER NEWS...

He's seen the future and it holds many wars.

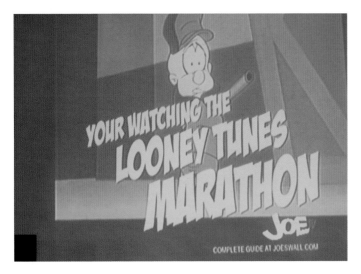

You're making our eyes hurt.

Bad grammar at its most widely visible.

"Legisil" is a new cream for something contagious. This square is sponsored by its creators.

THE SHEEN INTERVIEW

EXCLUSIVE: SHEEN TO SUE CBS

"THERE GONNA LOSE IN A COURT"

If they don't even know the "there"/"they're"/"their" distinction, they probably are going to lose in court.

Yes. Every viewer who saw this.

KIRK OCCUPIES
THE SENATE SEAT
FORMALLY HELD
BY BARAK OBAMA

NOW

The president had already been elected when this aired, so spelling his name wrong is pretty inexcusable. Ditto mistaking "formally" for "formerly."

Nine
∧
WORD OF MOUTH

START OFF RIGHT WITH ONE OR TWO OF THESE DELICIOUS APPETIZERS:

Onion Rings • *NEW* Clamstrips • Kettle-Cooked Chips

Fresh-Fried Jalapeño Coins • Cheese Sticks
NEW Zucchini • *NEW* Mushrooms

SINGLE ORDER - 2.99
DOUBLE COMBO - Pick any two - 5.79
Served with ranch, marinara, Thai Chili Sauce,
Campfire Sauce or tarter sauce

Would anyone like some tarter sauce with your jalapeño coins?

WE ARE OUT OF SPINACH UNTILL MONDAY
SORRY THE INCONVIENCE

Let's hope the spinach comes in by Monday, otherwise innocent customers will be subjected to this sign far longer.

Greek Omelette $7.99
Bacon Cheese omelette $7.99
Mushroom Cheese omelette $7.99
Spinach cheese omelette $7.99
Western Cheese omelette $8.99
Pepper Onion omelette $7.99
American cheese Omelette $6.99
Swiss cheese Omelette $6.99
Breakfast Wrap $7.99
Plain Omelette $5.99

All above served with Coffee Home Fries
and Toast. White eggs extra $1.00

Fried Cod
Chips $

All the abo
with tre
pickle,
fish
served w

"Coffee home fries" sounds like a kooky gourmet dish made by a bored chef. And brown eggs are less expensive than white ones.

ALL NESTLE COOKIE
PRODUCTS ARE
TEMPORARY OUT
OF STOCK

This appears to be at least an attempt at using an adverb, though it landed way off the mark.

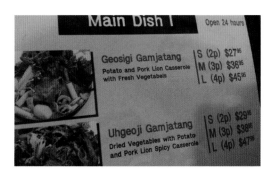

The King of the Jungle on sale here 24 hours a day. Also, make sure you get your daily serving of vegetabels.

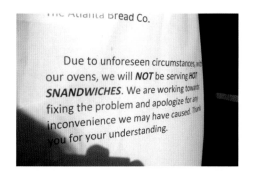

You'll probably never again see a sandwich so epically butchered.

The lemon shake-ups only have $1.50. Could you spare some change?

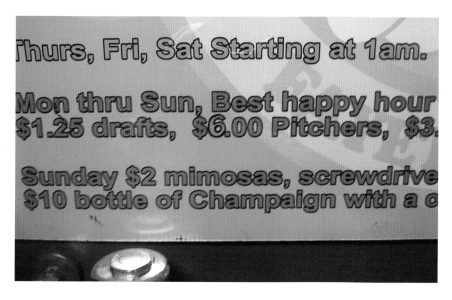

Thurs, Fri, Sat Starting at 1am.

Mon thru Sun, Best happy hour
$1.25 drafts, $6.00 Pitchers, $3.

Sunday $2 mimosas, screwdrive
$10 bottle of Champaign with a c

The Yankees would save a ton of money if they knew about these $6 pitchers. More important, though, is "champaign" a cross between a drink and a political candidate's efforts to get elected?

Fine Pub Dining

Billards

Billard: A duck that likes to play pool? A biller who's also a bastard? Sure.

Whoever wrote the contents of this fortune cookie did not foresee their mistake being captured on film and widely distributed.

There are no words. No really, one of these is not a real word.

If you never had any doubts about Taco Bell before, this should do it.

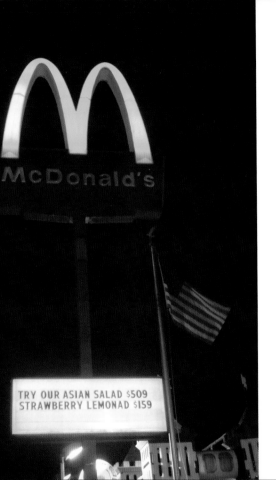

This could be correct. If all words were spelled phonetically.

If you're charging $159 for lemonade, you could at least afford to buy a vowel.

Oh good, the breakfast bur-
ritos got their coffee.

Although the food is Mexican, we're pretty sure the masterminds behind Chipotle speak English as a first language.

A less charitable reader would think this label refers to something scandalous.

(102)

2010/01/16

Once again, attack of the phonetic spellers!

Does this mean crumbled AND creamed? Interesting.

Since everybody knows what a "combo" is, perhaps the sign writer should have relied on that handy abbreviation. It's easier to get right.

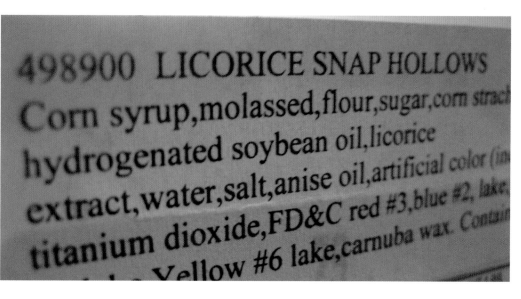

498900 LICORICE SNAP HOLLOWS

Corn syrup,molassed,flour,sugar,corn strach,
hydrogenated soybean oil,licorice
extract,water,salt,anise oil,artificial color (in
titanium dioxide,FD&C red #3,blue #2, lake,
Yellow #6 lake,carnuba wax. Contain

Oh, snap! Your licorice just got molassed.

Unnecessary apostrophes strike again! It seems they're multiplying.

Somebody was drinking and making signs.

Chockolate milk: chock full o' chocolate.

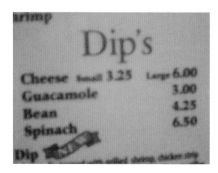

This dip owns cheese, guacamole, spinach, and a single bean. How lovely.

I'm afraid it's only infatuation. But how flattering.

Rise and shine! Use proper spelling!

Purshasing too many drinks may lead to slurred spelling.

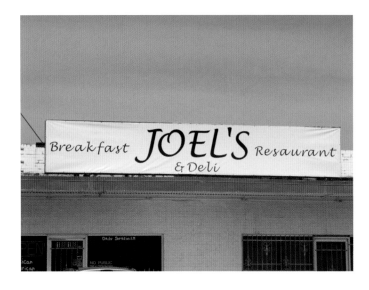

The correct possessive apostrophe is exciting but immediately canceled out by the misspelled "restaurant."

Ten

∧

DIRE WARNINGS

To all cashier / cooks i don't know who you are but if i find out you will be suspended for the first time and the second time you will be fired,if you are caught. When we get ice we do not put the bucket inside of the machine use the scoope please.

Anything menacing about this warning is entirely diminished by the second-grade spelling and punctuation. When we get ice, we use the scoope. Duh.

NEED A PASSPORT! APPLICATIONS ACCEPTED IN PERSONNEL OFFICE!

The arbitrary capitalization and punctuation in this sign make it come off like a demand. Get a passport…or else.

It's too bad that not knowing how to spell "disturb" undermines any authority communicated by the skull and crossbones. It's kind of like seeing a police officer driving a Segway.

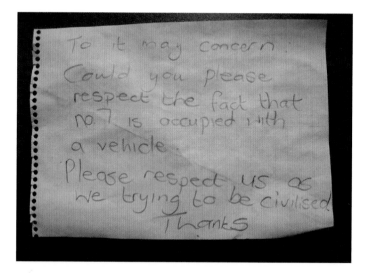

Your British neighbors are trying to be civilised this time. Don't make them get the hose.

Could they have meant "quite pleasing"?

Maybe "unattendent" means "with a terrible attendant."—like an infant or a drunken teenager or a DMV worker.

Maybe the author of this sign forgot a word at the end. "Stinger" would work.

When readers inevitably get angry at the lack of punctuation in this sign, its creator is responsible for subsequent damage.

You guys should reading the rules and regulation for parking in the community (5) Days and stay only can you PARK IN the visitors space your Red Honda Civic has to be move even if its to the next space, Pictures has to been taken AND Space marked by Towed company

"Pictures has to been taken and space marked by towed company." Got that? Good.

Quite please? Oh, quite thank you.

No, you are on camera.

PHOTO CREDITS

Rowena Aburto: 82 (left); Victoria Barranco: 90; Joshua Bertram: 44 (left), 100 (right); Ryan Billings: 107 (top); Patti Bondurant: 37, 38; Katharine Boyle: 13, 100 (left), 101; Mike Brabham: 109 (bottom); Elaine Braun-Keller: 21 (bottom right); Natalie Burke: 16 (bottom); Bri Catarino: 95 (bottom); Laura Chandler: 22 (top), 36 (right), 87 (bottom); David Chesler: 71; Joshua Christensen: 49; Amy Clawson Stier: 40 (top), 69, 93, 112 (bottom); Joe Collins: 99 (bottom left); Jolyn Curfman: 77, 86 (bottom); Siobhan Currell: 23 (top right), 47 (right), 50 (left), 61, 82 (right), 83, 84 (top), 108 (bottom); Ward Davis: 48 (left), 65, 66, 110; Maritxu de Alaiza: 103; Andrea Derrick: 3, 40 (bottom); Michael Douglas: 31, 57, 81 (top), 115; Andrea Dragna: 52 (top), 86 (top), 112 (top), 113 (top); Sarah Flory: 60 (bottom), 117 (left); Nathan Frandino: 106; Philip Gallegos: 116; Parks Gilbert: 59 (bottom); Abigail Grant: 67; Vikky Grey: 64 (middle); Elizabeth Gunnells: 11 (right); Amy Harshman: 94 (top); Tylene Headley: 23; Edward Jablonski: 27; Michael Kirchner: 15, 16 (top), 30, 45, 46, 58, 59 (top), 88, 89, 104 (bottom), 105; April Kolin: 20 (right), 52 (bottom); Jordana Lorraine Kotlus: 12, 43 (right); Jeremy J. Kruizenga: 75, 99 (bottom right); Jeanne LaSala: 43 (left); Annelies Lindemans: 4; Gemma Marshall: 73, 113 (bottom); Bill Mattinson: 95 (top); Brian McGarry: 7 (bottom); Celeste McCabe: 8, 9; Mac McCabe: 36 (left), 54, 78; Laurie Nash: 102 (right); Randy Neal: 107 (bottom); Tanay Nestico: 48 (right), 62, 63, 64 (top), 84 (bottom); Grace Nichols: 21 (bottom left); Sharon Nichols: 17, 47 (left), 50 (right), 108 (top); Katie Noles: 102 (left); Kaylee Nonnemacher: 44 (right), 78 (top); Lisa Nordyke: 114 (bottom); Nicole Pace: 81 (bottom right); Nicole Page: 23 (top left); David Parette: 10, 97; Jessica Pellman: 76; Tom Phillipson: 117 (right); Daniela Rapp: 14, 74, 81 (bottom left), 87 (top), 109 (top); Meigan Rath: 22 (bottom), 55, 56, 79, 80; Hilary Ray: 98; Francisco Reyes: 72; Brian Reynolds: 20 (left), 21 (top); Maria Photopulos: 29; Ashley Rooks: 5, 41, 53 (top), 70, 94 (bottom); Deanne Rowe: 11 (left); Gabriella Russotti: 28, 42; Peter Scoblic: 60 (top); Darren Spain: 96; Chandler Thomas: 26; Alaina Thonsgaard: 2, 34, 68, 92; Jenn Trommelen-Jones: 35; Holly Whitley: 53 (bottom), 99 (top), 114 (top); Martin Windolf: 104 (top)